بِسْمِ الله

In the name of Allah

This
BOOK
BELONGS to

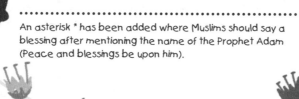

....

An asterisk * has been added where Muslims should say a
blessing after mentioning the name of the Prophet Adam
(Peace and blessings be upon him).

Prophet Adam and Wicked Iblis Activity Book

Published in 2018 by THE ISLAMIC FOUNDATION
An Imprint of KUBE PUBLISHING LTD
Tel +44 (0)1530 249230, Fax +44 (0)1530 249656
E-mail: info@kubepublishing.com
Website: www.kubepublishing.com

Text and illustrations © Ana Muslim Sdn Bhd, 2018
First published in Malaysia by Ana Muslim Sdn Bhd, 2017

• Writer : Saadah Taib
• Editor : Amalina Aida Abdul Rahim
• Illustrator : Shazana Rosli
• Cover design : Hazwanulhassan Mohd Nor
• Layout : Tan Peng Peng

A Cataloguing-in-Publication Data record for this book is available from the
British Library

ISBN 978-0-86037-639-2
Printed by Imak Ofset. Printed in Turkey.

It's the School Holidays

Find and circle the pink shirts.

The school holidays are here. Amani is going on a trip to the countryside with her class.

Along the way, Amani sees many beautiful things. Amani can see mountains, hills, waterfalls and lots of animals.

Name the animals.

'Mashallah! How wonderful,' says Amani.

The bus reaches the hilltop and Amani says, 'It's lovely here.' Mr Anwar smiles and says, 'Do you know that Prophet Adam once lived in a place even better than this?'

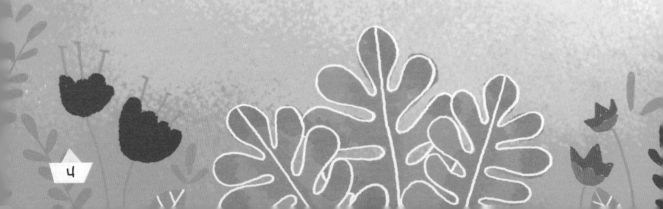

The First Man and Woman

Prophet Adam was the first human. He was created by Allah. Allah then created Hawwa, his wife. Prophet Adam and Hawwa were the first humans to live in Paradise and on Earth.

Name and draw other animals that live in the sea.

5

Prophet Adam Lived in Paradise

Prophet Adam and Hawwa lived in Paradise. Paradise is a beautiful place. They were happy. But somebody in Paradise was not.

Find these hidden letters.
EARTH

Iblis Was Jealous

Find these words: Adam, Hawwa, Hill, School, Pretty, Amani, Paradise and Book.

P	A	R	A	D	I	S	E
R	A	H	M	C	D	G	W
E	H	N	A	B	O	O	K
T	I	Q	N	W	P	R	A
T	L	R	I	F	W	D	B
Y	L	M	H	A	A	A	A
D	O	P	T	M	Y	K	V
J	S	C	H	O	O	L	B

Iblis lived in Paradise. Allah created him as well. He was jealous of Adam and Hawwa. He decided to trick Prophet Adam and Hawwa so that they would disobey Allah.

The Forbidden Tree

colour the fruits.

In Paradise, Allah said that Adam and Hawwa could eat anything - except the fruit from one tree.

Prophet Adam Disobeyed Allah

Complete the crossword puzzle.

```
              3.
               M
     2.         |
      C  □  □  □  D
               □
               |
    1. 5.      N
      S  □  N
         □
  6.     □
   □
4. E  □  R  □  H
   □
```

The wicked Iblis told Prophet Adam and Hawwa to eat fruit from the forbidden tree. And they did. Prophet Adam and Hawwa disobeyed Allah. They were ashamed.

The Answers: 1. Sun, 2. Cloud, 3. Moon, 4. Earth, 5. Star, 6. Sea.

9

Prophet Adam Repented

Prophet Adam and Hawwa asked Allah to forgive them. Allah is the All-Merciful. He forgave them for their mistake. But Prophet Adam and Hawwa had to leave Paradise.

Colour all the living things.

10

Life on Earth

Fill in the blanks.

B _ R _

_ R _ NG _

Allah sent Prophet Adam and Hawwa to live on Earth. They learned to farm and care for animals.

C _ T

CH _ CK _ N

Children of Prophet Adam

Prophet Adam and Hawwa were blessed with many children. Soon those children had children.

How many corns are there?

Humankind

Find these objects.

All human beings are the children of Prophet Adam and Hawwa. Every man and woman, boy and girl.

'In the eyes of Allah, are we all created equal Mr Anwar?" asks Amani.
'That's right Amani. But Allah *really* loves those who do good and believe in Him.' Mr Anwar says.

The Earth

Allah wants humans to take care of the earth.
Let's fill it with peace and keep it tidy.

What can you name in the picture?

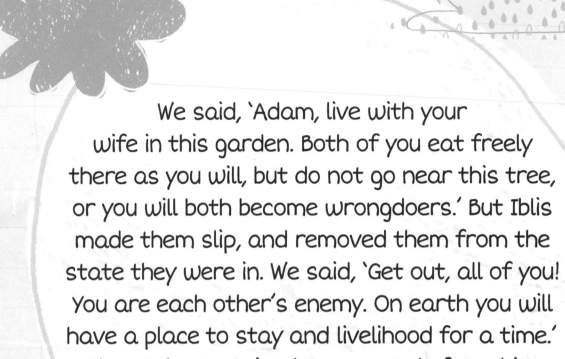

We said, 'Adam, live with your wife in this garden. Both of you eat freely there as you will, but do not go near this tree, or you will both become wrongdoers.' But Iblis made them slip, and removed them from the state they were in. We said, 'Get out, all of you! You are each other's enemy. On earth you will have a place to stay and livelihood for a time.' Then Adam received some words from his Lord and He accepted his repentance: He is the Ever Relenting, the Most Merciful.

(Surah al-Baqarah 2:35-36)